Welcome, little one!

Let's explore together!

Smiling moon
in the sky!

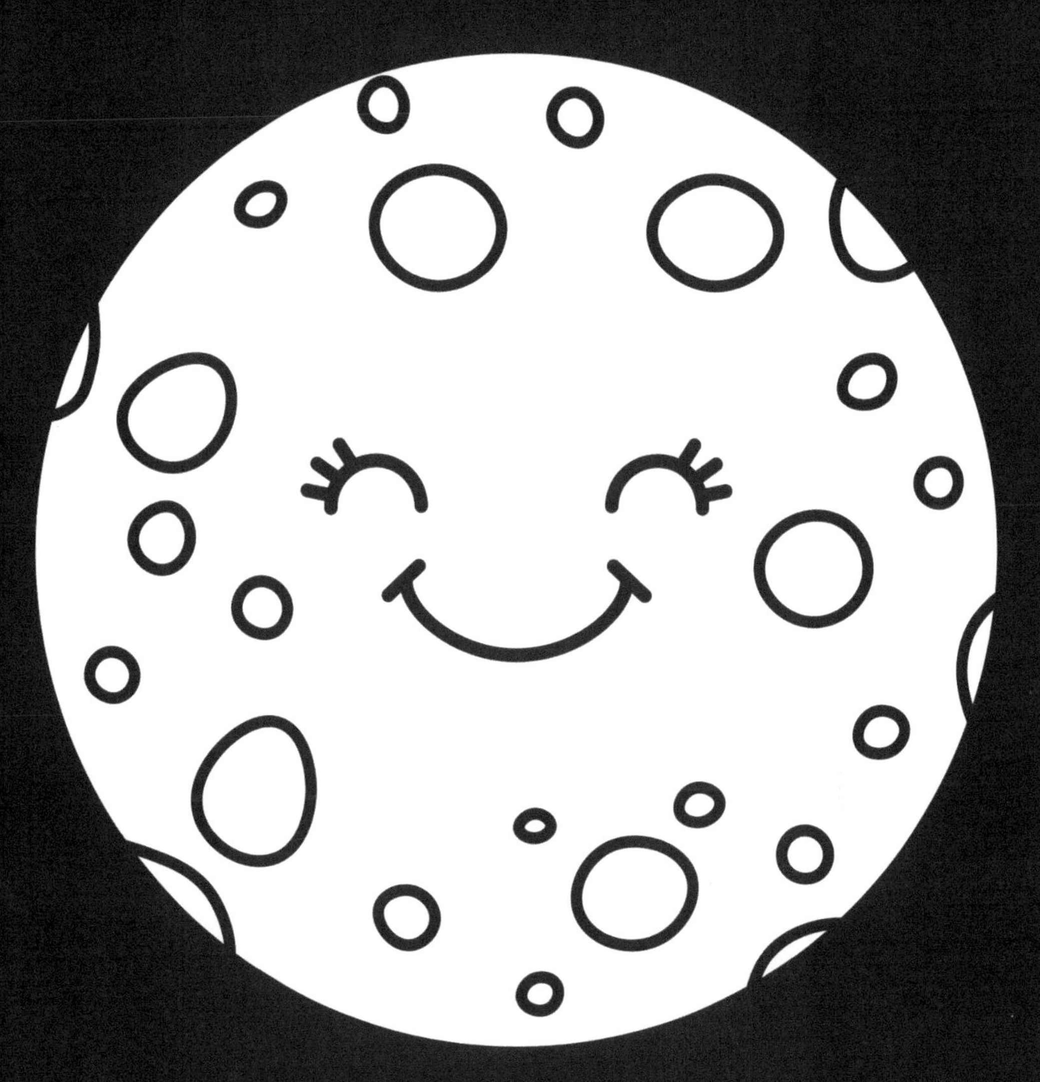

Buzz, buzz!
A happy bee!

Hello,
sunshine!

Smiling banana
says hi!

Twinkle, twinkle, little star!

Sleepy elephant
takes a nap!

Little tree with falling leaves!

A pretty flower
blooms!

Wiggly worm in
an apple!

A
is for adorable!

Wise little owl
says hello!